GW00949969

Methuen/Moonlight
First published 1983 by Editions Gallimard
First published 1984 in Great Britain by Methuen
Children's Books Ltd, 11 New Fetter Lane, London EC4
in association with Moonlight Publishing Ltd,
131 Kensington Church Street, London W8
Illustrations © 1983 by Editions Gallimard
English text and selection of poems © 1984
by Moonlight Publishing Ltd

Printed in Italy by La Editoriale Libraria

ISBN 0 907144 60 8

WINTER

DISCOVERERS

by Laurence Ottenheimer
adapted and edited by Alex Campbell
illustrations by Danièle Bour

methuen ● moonlight

Here's a song –
stags give tongue
winter snows
summer goes.

Cold now girds
wings of birds
icy time –
that's my rime.

Irish song

December

Winter begins at the winter solstice. This is the shortest day of the year. It occurs on 21 or 22 December.

22 When the days begin to lengthen, Then the cold begins to strengthen.

23

24 **Christmas Eve**

On 25 December the ancient Romans celebrated the feast of the winter solstice, after which days start growing longer.

Now on the same day Christians all over the world celebrate the birth of Jesus Christ. And we number the years of our calendar from the year of his birth.

The exact day of Christ's birth is in fact unknown. But in the fourth century the Christian Church decided to celebrate it on 25 December and so converted the old Roman feast into a Christian one: Christmas.

And all the bells on earth shall ring
On Christmas Day in the morning.
Old carol

Before the paling of the stars,
Before the winter morn,
Before the earliest cockcrow,
Jesus Christ was born.

Christina Rossetti

7

Green under frost
Green under snow
Green under tinsel
Glitter and glow
Appled with baubles
Silver and gold
Spangled with fire
Warm over cold

Laurence Smith

Dame get up and bake your pies On Christmas Day in the morning.

25 Christmas Day

The Christmas Tree was a German custom, introduced to the royal family in Windsor Castle in 1841 by Prince Albert, Queen Victoria's husband. But from earliest times, evergreens, like the fir tree, which stay green all winter long, have been considered magical.

Trees, presents and decorations are customs that go back a very long way. The Romans decorated trees with candles and gave presents at the *Saturnalia*, a wild festival held at the end of the year in honour of Saturn, god of agriculture.

Now Christians give presents to celebrate the birth of Christ. Each country has its special traditions. While English children hang up stockings for Father Christmas, Spanish children put out shoes for the Three Kings.

Saint Nicholas, the patron saint of children, brings presents in Holland on his feast day, 6 December. Dutch children put out wooden clogs filled with hay and carrots for his horse.

Saint Nicholas was a bishop who lived in Asia in the fourth century. He is often pictured with three children in a tub and an old legend tells how he saved them from death . . .

The Legend of Saint Nicholas

There were once three little children who wandered so far into the fields that by nightfall they were completely lost and knocked at the nearest door. 'Mr Butcher, may we spend the night?' they asked.

'Come in, come in, little children,' said the butcher, 'I have plenty of room.' No sooner had they stepped inside, than he chopped them into little pieces and put them into a pickling tub.

Seven years came and went, when St. Nicholas happened to pass by and knocked at the door. 'Mr. Butcher, may I spend the night?' he said.

'Come in, come in, St. Nicholas,' said the butcher, 'I have plenty of room.'

'I want some of the pickled meat,' said St. Nicholas, 'that you have had in your tub for seven years.' Hearing these words the butcher fled from the house in terror. Then St. Nicholas stretched out three fingers and called: 'Wake up, little children.'

The three children came to life and looked out of the tub.

The first said: 'I had a good night's sleep.'

The second said: 'So did I.'

And the smallest added: 'I dreamed I was in heaven.'

*The Young New Year has come so soon
I wonder where the Old Years go?
To some dim land behind the moon
Where starlight glimmers, pale and low.*   Anon.

26 Boxing Day and St Stephen

27
28   *Ha wish you a merry
Chresamus,
An a happy new year,
A pantry full a' good rost beef,
And a barril full a' beer.* Anon.
29

30

31   **New Year's Eve**

*Old One, lie down,
Your journey is done,
Little New Year
Will rise with the sun.*
Eleanor Farjeon

11

January

At the beginning of January sunrise is at about 8.05 and sunset at about 16.00. Each day the sun rises about 1 minute earlier and sets over 1 minute later than the day before.

Shepherd, good shepherd, come in from the wet, The New Year has risen, the Old Year has set.

Eleanor Farjeon

1 New Year's Day

2 Thirty days hath September, April, June and November;

3 All the rest have 31, Excepting February alone,

4 And that has 28 days clear and 29 in each Leap Year.

31 January
28/29 February
31 March
30 April
31 May
30 June
31 July
31 August
30 September
31 October
30 November
31 October

Count the months along your knuckles and the dips between: the months that fall on the knuckles are long (31 days); the months in the dips are short (28, 29 or 30 days).

We three Kings of Orient are,
Bearing gifts we traverse afar.

Carol

5

6 **Epiphany**
Feast of the Three Kings

And lo, the star which they saw in the east went before them, till it came and stood where the young child was . . . And when they were come into the house, they saw the young child with Mary, his mother, and fell down and worshipped him: and when they had opened their treasures they presented unto him gifts: gold, and frankincense, and myrrh. (Matthew II 9)

Now, now,
the mirth comes
With the cake
full of plums,
Where bean's
the king
of the sport here.

Robert Herrick

Once Christmas celebrations lasted for twelve days and Epiphany was known as **Twelfth Night.** It was a custom to make a Twelfth Cake with a bean inside: whoever found the bean was king for the day, the Bean King. This is still done in France where little china figures are hidden in the cake.

I'm glad we have wood in store awhile
For soon we must shut the door awhile,
As winterly winds may roar awhile,
And scatter the whirling snow.

William Barnes

7 Partly work and partly play
You must on St Distaff's Day.

8

9 *The morning after winter*
when bitter weather came,

10 *the chickadee was cheery –*
as cheery as his name,

11 *but I should think he'd like a*
pair of earmuffs, all the same.

Aileen Fisher

12

13

14 St Hilary

The days are short,
The sun a spark
Hung thin between
The dark and dark.

John Updike

15

16 *January brings the snow*
Makes our feet and fingers glow.

17 Sara Coleridge

18

19 What is it that freezeth never?
Hot water.

If January could,
he would be a summer month
Greek proverb

20

21 Fair St Agnes, play thy part,
And send to me my own sweetheart.

22

23

24 If St Paul's day be fair and clear,
It does betide a happy year;

25 But if by chance it then should rain,
It will make dear all kinds of grain.

26

27

28 The last twelve days of January,
rule the weather for the whole year.

29

30

31 **New Year's Eve**
Hogmanay in Scotland

A summerish January,
a winterish spring.

*Fat snowy foot
steps
Track the floor.
Milk bottles burst
Outside the door.*
John Updike

February

February is the shortest month of the year. It has 28 days, but 29 days in Leap Year, which comes every fourth year whose number can be divided by 4.

At the beginning of February sunrise is at about 7.40 and sunset at about 16.45. Each day the sun rises about 2 minutes earlier and sets about 2 minutes later.

Pancake Day

In the Middle Ages people were forbidden to eat meat, milk and eggs during **Lent,** the 40 days leading up to Easter. They used up their eggs and milk by making pancakes on the day before Ash Wednesday, when Lent began. So this day got the name Pancake Day.

The days before Lent were a time of carnival, when people danced in the streets wearing fancy dress and masks. Some places, such as Venice, still hold carnivals before Lent.

Another name for Pancake Day is Shrove Tuesday: on this day people were 'shriven', or confessed their sins. But shroving then came to mean making merry before Lent. People made shrove cakes to give children.

Snick, snock, the pan's
hot,
We be come
a-shroving:
Please to gie us
summat,
Summat's better'n
nothin'

Anon.

Pancake Day, Pancake Day,
If you don't give us a holiday,
We'll all run away.

1

2

Candlemas

Candlemas is the feast of light, the day when candles were brought to church to be blessed, then carried through the streets in procession.

In France it is a custom to make pancakes at Candlemas. Pancakes have the shape of the new moon: the last moon of winter which heralded the spring. People wished on them for a good harvest.

If Candlemas Day be fair and bright,
Winter will have another flight;
But if Candlemas Day bring
clouds and rain,
Winter is gone and will not come again.

Party Pancakes:
Put 500 g of flour in a big bowl. Whisk in 6 eggs, then 3 tablespoons sugar. Gradually add ¾l milk, ¼l water and 100 g melted butter. Let the batter rest for an hour.

Mix a pancake,
Stir a pancake,
Pop it in the pan.
Fry the pancake,
Toss the pancake,
Catch it if you can.

Christina Rossetti

The men of the East
  Are picking their geese,
    And sending their feathers here away,
        there away. Anon

3 February fill the dyke,
Be it black or be it white.

4

5

6 St Dorothea gives the most snow.

7

8 *Summer-swollen doorjambs settle,*
Ponds and puddles turn to metal,

9 *Skater whoops in frisky fettle,*
Golf-club stingeth like a nettle,

10 *Radiator sings like kettle,*
Hearth is popocatapetl.

Ogden Nash

11

12

13

14 **Saint Valentine's Day,** a custom
which goes back to Roman times.

Good morrow Valentine I'll be yours
If you'll be mine Valentine   Anon

18

15	
16	Winter's back breaks about the middle of February.
17	*If I were a bear,* *And a big bear too,*
18	*I shouldn't much care* *If it froze or snew;*
19	*I shouldn't much mind* *If it snowed or friz –*
20	*I'd be all fur-lined* *With a coat like his!* A.A.Milne
21	
22	
23	*The fire is winter's fruit* Arab proverb
24	
25	When the cat in February lies in the sun, she will creep behind the stove in March.
26	
27	
28	*February brings the rain* *Thaws the frozen lake again.* Sara Coleridge
29	

March

At the beginning of March, sunrise is at about 6.50 and sunset at about 17.40. Each day the sun rises about 2 minutes earlier and sets about 2 minutes later than the day before.

March, many weathers.

Saying

1 St David's Day, celebrated by the Welsh.

2 St David and Chad,
Sow pease good or bad.

3 In March fools go barefoot.
French proverb

4 *March winds and April showers
Bring forth May flowers.*

5

6

7

8 In March
The birds begin to search.

9

March, black ram,
Comes in like a lion,
and goes out like a lamb.

Saying

10

11 *A blue day,*
a blue jay

12 *and a good beginning.*
One crow,

13 *melting snow –*
spring's winning!

Elizabeth Coatsworth

14

15

16

In March, all sorts of weather,
Winds wait for you round every
corner,
Sun shines, hailstones the moment
after,
Hoar frost on gardens, drizzly
mornings.

In March, all sorts of colours,
Grey skies and water, violets in
woodlands,
Greenfinches on far greener
branches,
Speckled trout rising, first
butterflies.

Leonard Clark

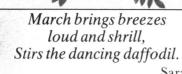

*March brings breezes
loud and shrill,
Stirs the dancing daffodil.*

Sara Coleridge

17 St. Patrick's Day, celebrated by the Irish.

18 *There goes Winter sloshing off with puddles in his tracks.*

19 *Here comes Spring on roller skates with jumping ropes and jacks.*

Aileen Fisher

20

21 **First day of Spring**

Winter ends at the spring or vernal equinox, when day and night are the same length. This occurs on 20 or 21 March.

The northern and southern hemispheres of the world have opposite seasons to each other. So as spring is beginning for us, autumn is beginning in Australia.

*January brings burning heat,
and red dust dims the sun.
February has gifts of fruit,
but says the summer's done.
Windy March brings ripened grapes,
and blows the autumn in.*

Irene Gough

A winter day 100 years ago . . .

It was an intense frost. I sat down in my bath upon a sheet of thick ice which broke in the middle into large pieces whilst sharp points and jagged edges stuck all round the sides of the tub like 'chevaux de frise' (barbed wire), not particularly comforting to the thighs and loins, for the keen ice cut like broken glass. The ice water stung and scorched like fire. I had to collect the floating pieces of ice and pile them on a chair before I could use the sponge and then I had to thaw the sponge in my hands for it was a mass of ice. The morning was most brilliant. Walked to the Sunday School with Gibbins and the road sparkled with millions of rainbows, the seven colours gleaming in every glittering point of hoar frost. The church was very cold in spite of two roaring stove fires.

Christmas Day 1870, from the
Diary of Rev. Francis Kilvert

The moving Earth

1 Summer solstice (21 June).
The longest day and beginning of summer in the northern hemisphere.
The shortest day and beginning of winter in the southern hemisphere.

2 Autumn equinox (22 or 23 September).
Day and night are the same length in both hemispheres.

Day and Night

We say that the sun rises in the east and sets in the west, because it appears to move across the sky during the day. In fact it is the earth that moves.

Imagine a line running through the earth from north to south pole. This is the earth's axis, which tilts to one side in relation to the sun. Every 24 hours the earth spins once on its axis: each part of the world in turn passes through the sun's light, which is day, then through the sun's shadow, which is night.

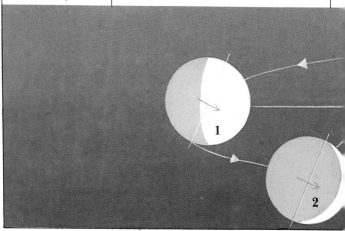

*In winter I get up at night
And dress by yellow candle-light;
In summer, quite the other way,
    I have to go to bed by day.* R. L. Stevenson

Winter and summer

Every 365 days, which is our year, the earth travels once round the sun. It tilts to one side as it travels, which causes the change of the seasons. First one hemisphere and then the other leans closer to the sun.

When the northern hemisphere tilts towards the sun we get more daylight and heat: it is summer.

When the northern hemisphere tilts away from the sun we get less daylight and heat: it is winter.

There are two times in the year when neither hemisphere points towards the sun and day and night are exactly equal. These are the spring and autumn equinoxes.

3 Winter solstice (22 December) The shortest day and beginning of winter in the northern hemisphere. The longest day and beginning of summer in the southern hemisphere.

4 Spring equinox (20 or 21 March) Day and night are the same length in both hemispheres.

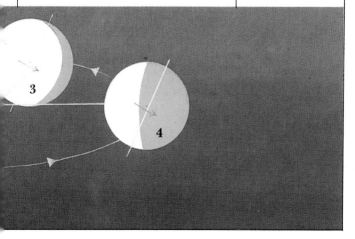

Stars in the winter sky

Star light,
star bright,
First star
I see tonight...

1 Pegasus
The Winged Horse
2 Cepheus
3 Casseopeia
4 Polaris
5 Ursa Minor
– the Little Bear
6 Ursa Major
– the Great Bear
7 The Plough
8 Draco
– the Dragon
9 Cygnus
– the Swan

A clear winter night when the moon is new is a good time for star-watching.

Each night, as the Earth turns on its axis, the stars seem to move from east to west across the sky. And at each season, as the earth moves round the sun, they appear in different positions in the sky.

Stars are huge balls of burning gases, like our sun. They look tiny because they are so far away.

Looking north

The winter falls; the frozen rut
Is bound with silver bars,
The snowdrift heaps against the hut
And night is pierced with stars.   Coventry Patmore

Light travels very fast: nearly 300,000,000 km in one second. It takes over four years for the light from the nearest stars (except the sun) to reach us.

When you look at Andromeda, the light you see has been travelling for 2,200,000 years! This is the furthest constellation (or group of stars) which can be seen without a telescope.

Looking south

...I wish I may,
I wish I might,
Have the wish
I wish tonight.
                    Anon.

1 Gemini
  – The Twins
2 Auriga
  – The Waggoner
3 The Triangle
4 Andromeda
5 Taurus
  – The Bull
6 Cetus
  – The Whale
7 Eridanus
8 Orion
9 Canis Major

Red sun

Red sky at night,
Shepherd's delight.

The winter sun often looks red on the horizon. In fact it is white, but white light is made up of many colours. We can see this when the sun shines on a rainy day: as its white rays pass through raindrops they split up into a rainbow, showing all the colours of the spectrum.

When the sky looks blue, it is because specks of dust floating in the air catch and reflect the blue rays in sunlight and let other rays go past. The light that reaches us looks yellow.

In the morning and evening, when the sun is low in the sky, its rays must travel farther to reach us. The longer rays in the spectrum, like blue and green, are stopped and the shorter red rays get through. A clear sky and a bright sunset usually mean fine weather the following day.

Late lies the wintery sun a-bed,
A frosty, fiery sleepy-head;
Blinks but an hour or two; and then,
A blood-red orange, sets again.
                                   R. L Stevenson

New moon, full moon

The moon, which is made of rock, shines because it reflects the sun's light.

The moon travels round the Earth as the Earth travels round the sun. The three planets are always changing position in relation to each other.

When the moon is between the Earth and sun we cannot see it at night. As it moves round the Earth away from the sun we begin to see a crescent. It grows a little each night until the Earth is placed between the moon and sun and the full moon appears. Then we see a little less of the moon each night until it arrives between sun and Earth and disappears from view again.

The moon's journey round the Earth takes one month.

full moon

first quarter

last quarter

The wind

Wind is air moving.

Air rises when it is warmed, pushing the cooler air downwards to take its place. The land and the sea store heat from the sun and give it off, warming the air near them. At the same time, warm air rising loses its heat and grows cooler. So there is a continual movement.

Cold winds generally blow from the north, warm ones from the south. Sea winds warm the land in winter and cool it in summer. This is because the sea itself gets warm or cool more slowly than the land.

*Who has seen the
    wind?
Neither I nor you:
But when the leaves
    hang trembling
The wind is
    passing through.
Who has seen the
    wind?
Neither you nor I:
But when the trees
    bow down their
    heads
The wind is
    passing by.*

Christina Rossetti

*I can get through a doorway
    without any key,
And strip the leaves from
    the great oak tree.*

James Reeves

30

Voiceless it cries,
Wingless flutters,
Toothless bites,
Mouthless mutters.   Tolkien

The wind's quarters

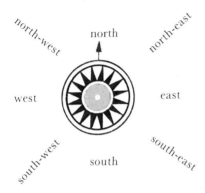

north-west   north   north-east

west   east

south-west   south   south-east

I saw you toss the
kites on high
And blow the birds
about the sky . . .
R. L. Stevenson

When the wind is in the East,
It's neither good for man nor
*   beast,*
When the wind is in the North,
The skilful fisher goes not
*   forth.*
When the wind is in the South,
It blows the bait in the fish's
*   mouth.*
When the wind is in the West,
Then it is at its very best.
    Proverb

Snowfall at dusk

No breath of wind,
No gleam of sun –
Still the white snow
Whirls softly down –
Twig and bough
And blade and thorn
All in an icy
Quiet, forlorn.
Whispering, rustling,
Through the air,
On sill and stone,
Roof - everywhere,
It heaps its powdery
Crystal flakes,
Of every tree
A mountain makes;
Till pale and faint
At shut of day,
Stoops from the West
One wintry ray.

Walter de la Mare

Snow

Snow forms from tiny drops of water floating in the clouds. When the temperature falls below 0°c the droplets of water turn into tiny icicles which join together and build up into snow-crystals.

Each snow-crystal has its own unique design but all are perfectly symmetrical and six-pointed. Some are prism-shaped. Most are like stars.

A snow year, a rich year.

Snowflakes

On a very still day ice-crystals fall one by one. But when there is movement in the air they stick to each other as they fall, forming snowflakes, which can be small or large.

A snowflake consists of a little ice and a lot of air trapped among the icicles: like a pillow full of feathers with air trapped among the feathers.

Winter is the king of showmen,
Turning tree stumps into snow men
And houses into birthday cakes
And spreading sugar over lakes.
Smooth and clean and frosty white,
The world looks good enough to
*   bite.*
That's the season to be young,
Catching snowflakes on your
*   tongue.*
Snow is snowy when it's snowing
I'm sorry it's slushy when it's going.
Ogden Nash

You can build with snow. Eskimoes make igloos out of it. But it has to be the right kind of snow, not too icy, or too wet. Eskimoes have a different word for each type of snow.

One without looks in tonight
Through the curtain-chink
From the sheet of glistening white;
One without looks in tonight
As we sit and think
By the fender brink.

We do not discern those eyes
Watching in the snow;
Lit by lamps of rosy dyes
We do not discern those eyes,
Wondering, aglow,
Fourfooted, tiptoe.

Thomas Hardy

Frost

After a freezing winter night, you may wake up to find the world outside encrusted in white and patterns of ice-crystals covering your window pane. This is frost.

Frost is a fine layer of ice which forms from water in the air. Water is in the air in the form of invisible vapour. And mist and fog are made of tiny floating drops of water which are too light to fall – until, in freezing temperatures, they are deposited as crystals of ice on everything they touch.

The frosted window shows tall white ferns, and trees, and rivers with twists and turns, and strange white forests with flowers of ice . . . wish I could walk in a place that nice.

Aileen Fisher

Hail and ice, and ice and hail,
Water frozen in the pail,
See the robins, brown and red
They are waiting to be fed.
Poor dears; battling in the gale!
Hail and ice, and ice and hail.

Katherine Mansfield

Hailstorms

Hail is frozen raindrops. They form at very high altitudes, where the air is very cold.

Before a storm the air close to the ground grows warm and rushes upwards with enormous force. Clouds floating at 1000–3000 metres may be suddenly driven as high as 15000 metres by the wind. The tiny drops of water which make up the clouds merge into each other and freeze, becoming hailstones.

Hailstones grow in size as they are whirled up and down in the cloud and more water drops freeze round them.

The Big Freeze

Wherever temperatures fall below 0°c, water freezes. And as it turns to ice it expands. This means that it takes up more room. Water can burst pipes when it freezes inside them. It can split rock when it freezes down cracks in a rock.

Lives in winter,
Dies in summer
And grows with its
root upwards.

icicle

When water freezes as it drips, it forms icicles. These icicles are called *stalactites*.

Sometimes, when water drips, the drops freeze one by one as they hit the ground. They build up beautiful columns of ice, growing upwards. They are called *stalagmites*.

There is a little rhyme to help remember which is which:

Mites grow up,
Tights come down.

Snow wind-whipt to ice
Under a hard sun:
Stream-runnels curdled hoar
Crackle, cannot run.   Richard Hughes

How snow turns into ice

New-fallen snow is light because of all the air that is caught inside snowflakes. But when snow lies thick on the ground it is pressed down by its own weight, and if the weather grows warmer, some of the snow melts. In both cases, the air is driven out, the snow is compressed and becomes hard. If it freezes again, the little ice crystals, which have been squashed together, merge and turn into ice.

Plants in the freeze

Inside them, plants have sap, which is water mixed with food. It keeps them alive. When it is very cold, the sap freezes, expanding and bursting the little vessels through which it flows. The plant dies.

The frozen pond

*The Sun's an
iceberg
In the sky.
In solid freeze
The fishes lie.*

Ted Hughes

Ice forms first on the surface of the pond. It is lighter than water and floats on it, as an ice cube does in a drink.

The longer it freezes, the thicker the layer of ice becomes. But the water beneath it stays at 4°C, warm enough for fish to stay alive.

A pike

If Winter comes, can Spring be far behind?

P. B. Shelley

Food is scarce in winter for fish, as for all wild creatures. But many can survive a long time without eating.

The pike is normally the tiger of fresh water: it devours fish, frogs, young birds, water voles. But in winter it rests sluggishly at the bottom of the pond, flicking its tail now and then to keep warm. For once, other fish can live in peace.

When it thaws, ice to water is reconciled.

Teitoku

Tracks and footprints

Sometimes animals leave tracks in the snow or on muddy ground. If you study them closely you may build up a story of what was happening when the animals left their footprints – sheep sheltering in a storm, a fox chasing a rabbit . . .

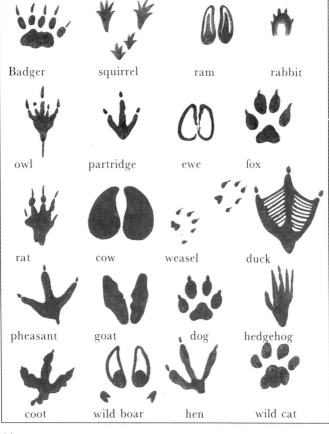

Badger squirrel ram rabbit

owl partridge ewe fox

rat cow weasel duck

pheasant goat dog hedgehog

coot wild boar hen wild cat

Winter woods are lonely and bare.
The whistling winds rush by,
There is no person anywhere,
Only the white owls fly,
And the thieving foxes dare.
Leonard Clark

Snug and warm

Small mammals need to shelter from the cold weather. In the autumn they dig tunnels just under the surface of the ground, and make themselves nests which they pack with grass and grain, food for the hard times ahead. If they run out of food, they burrow upwards and gnaw at the roots of plants, or tunnel under the snow to find green shoots. Then they return to their snug nests.

Fieldmouse, dormouse, shrew

The tiny pigmy shrew, only a few centimetres long, is the smallest of all mammals. Because it is so small it gets cold quickly and needs to eat every 3 hours in order to survive in winter.

White as snow

Some animals change colour from season to season, matching the changes in the scenery round them. This makes it harder for their enemies – and prey – to spot them.

As the days grow short, **stoats,** or **ermines,** living in the north, where winters are snowy, start to turn white. They become the colour of snow, except for the tips of their tails which are black all year round. These black-tipped white tails used to be much prized as a trimming for grand cloaks and crowns. In very cold weather stoats' fur grows extra thick. They replace it in spring with a new coat of brown fur.

In summer the **ptarmigan's** feathers are grey-brown, like the rocks of the hills and mountains where it lives. But it grows a coat of white feathers for the winter: even the sharp eyes of its predators have difficulty spotting it in the snow. It digs itself a shelter, like a little igloo in the snow.

The **blue mountain hare** is bluish grey in summer. Through the autumn and winter it gradually changes to white. In winter it hollows out a shelter in the snow and survives by eating heather.

Tonight has no moon,
no food for the pilgrim;
the fruit tree is bare,
the rose bush a thorn
and the ground bitter with stones.

But the mole sleeps, and the hedgehog
lies curled in a womb of leaves,
the bean and the wheat-seed
hug their germs in the earth
and the stream moves under the ice.

Laurie Lee

A long winter's night

Some animals hibernate: they sleep through the cold of winter, when food is scarce, and wake up in the spring.

During hibernation their body temperature drops, their heart beats very slowly and they scarcely breathe. They live on the stores of fat that their bodies built up in summer.

The North American **marmot** hibernates longer than any other animal, for 8 months of the year.

The hedgehog rolls itself into a ball to sleep. You can sometimes hear it snoring under a pile of leaves.

The happiness of hedgehogs
Lies in complete repose.
They spend the months of winter
In a long delicious doze.

E. V. Rieu

49

Winter Feeding

Wild animals that do not hibernate have a hard time surviving in winter. To protect themselves from the cold the stoat, weasel and marten grow thicker coats. Food is scarce, so they have to travel long distances as they hunt for prey.

The weasel hunts at night, slinking hungrily after voles and fieldmice in their holes underground.

The **pine marten** may cover many kilometres hunting by night. It eats squirrels, chasing them relentlessly through the snowy woods. It is a good climber and by day rests in the upper branches of a tree.

> *Cold, delicately as the dark snow*
> *The fox's nose touches twig, leaf.*
>
> Ted Hughes

Some animals store food in the autumn for the winter months. **Woodmice** take nuts, berries and seeds to their nests. **Jays** bury acorns.

Squirrels collect pine cones, grain, mushrooms, acorns, beech and hazel nuts. They hide them in holes or bury them in the ground not far from their nests. And on fine winter days they come out to fetch them. But often they forget where they have hidden their stores!

A squirrel's nest is called a *drey*. It is made of sticks, bark and moss and has a roof and entrance at the side. Squirrels occasionally take long naps at home in winter.

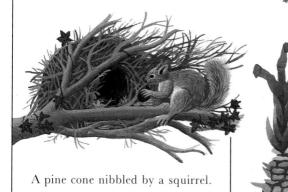

A pine cone nibbled by a squirrel.

Nibblers of nuts

In winter, when other food is scarce, hazelnuts are a favourite of many small animals. And each one has its own way of opening the shell.

The squirrel bites a little hole at the top of the nut. Then, with its lower incisors, it prises open the shell which splits in two. Young squirrels have to practise before they learn the technique.

Where's his supper?
In the shell.
Snappy cracky,
Out it fell.

Anon

The city mouse eats bread and cheese;
The garden mouse eats what it can;
We will not grudge him seeds and stocks,
Poor little timid furry man.   Christina Rossetti

The vole gnaws the end of the nut.

The nuthatch lodges the hazelnut in a crack in the tree and pierces the shell with sharp pecks of its beak.

The mouse nibbles through the side of the shell.

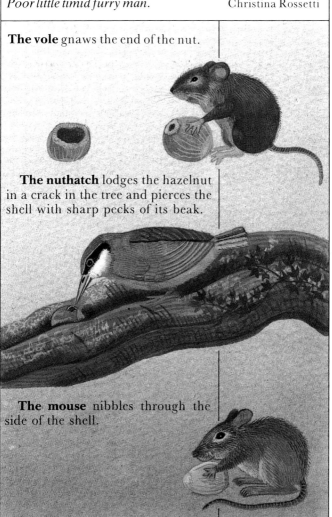

The badger

The badger eats roots, fruit, honey, slugs, snails, worms, insects, snakes, young birds and rabbits. By the autumn it is so plump that it can hardly run. The stores of fat it builds up keep it alive through the winter.

In very cold countries the badger hibernates. In England it only sleeps for short periods. It spends the winter in its underground burrow called a *set*. There it makes a comfortable bed of soft moss, dried leaves and grass. The entrance to the set gives onto a long passage leading to a large chamber deep under the ground. As the badger spends a lot of time at home it makes several chambers, each with an exit and ventilation. In winter, when it does not need so much space, it lets other badgers or foxes or rabbits use some of the chambers.

The badger is a wary animal and difficult to see. In winter it comes out now and again to drink, preferring to do so in the evening. Except in times of danger, it always uses the same entrance.

Baby badgers, born in the winter or early spring, often have regular playgrounds where the young from several sets will meet and play together.

White is my neck, head yellow, sides
The same. Weapons I wear, am
   hurried, and along
My back as on my cheek stands hair.
   Two ears
Above my eyes, through greenest
   grass
On claws I go . . . Working with
   forefeet
A way through the steep hill, with ease
   I shall
Lead out my dears through the down
By a tunnel in secret.

Geoffrey Grigson

The mole

*Don't you feel
sorry
for grubby old
moles,
always in tunnels,
always in holes.*
Aileen Fisher

The mole spends most of its life underground. All year long, it digs tunnels with its paws, which are shaped like little shovels. As it works it throws up heaps of earth, which we call molehills.

The mole eats worms, catching

56

So he scraped and scratched and scrabbled and scrooged, and then he scrooged again and scrabbled and scratched and scraped, working busily with his little paws.
Kenneth Grahame *(Wind in the Willows)*

them in the autumn and storing them in an underground chamber for the winter. As it likes to eat them alive, it bites their heads off to stop them escaping, which does not kill them. But if the mole leaves them too long, the worms grow a new head and wriggle away to freedom.

The Ants
and the Grasshopper

It was winter-time and the ants' store of grain had got wet, so they were laying it out to dry. A hungry grasshopper asked the ants for food, for it was near death.

'Why did you not gather food in the summer, like us?' asked the ants.

'I hadn't time,' replied the grasshopper. 'I was too busy dancing, singing, and making music.'

The ants laughed at the grasshopper and said, 'Very well, since you piped in the summer, now you must dance the winter away.'

Aesop
(Fable, trans. Harold Jones)

Insects

Many insects die in cold weather. Some, though, sleep through the winter buried in the earth or hidden in cocoons.

The queen bee and her workers huddle together in the hive, feeding on the honey they made in the summer, and hardly moving. If they do not have enough honey, the bee-keeper feeds them with sugar and water syrup. To keep out the cold, he wraps the hive in straw or leaves.

The colorado beetle adores eating potato leaves and can do great damage. Unfortunately because it has a nasty taste, birds leave it alone. It seems to have an inner clock: as soon as there are under 15 hours of daylight, it eats as much as it can, buries itself and goes to sleep.

The processionary caterpillar spins a nest of white silk on a pine tree and spends the winter there, feeding on pine needles. In spring the caterpillars emerge from their cocoons and crawl to the ground in long lines.

The ladybird sleeps all winter in a sheltered place: under the bark of a tree or in a crack in a window frame.

Birds of the night

Owls generally hunt by night and rest by day. But scarcity of prey in winter can drive them to hunt in the daytime as well. They feed on rodents, small birds and sometimes insects and fish, catching them in their sharp and powerful claws.

The tawny owl, also known as the brown or wood owl, lives in parks and other wooded places. If it is caught out in daylight it is often mobbed by noisy flocks of the small birds which go in terror of it at night.

The barn owl has, like all owls, very soft feathers which muffle the sound of its wings as it flies. It swoops almost soundlessly on its victims. It is also called the **screech owl** because of its shrieking cry. It nests in barns, clock towers and abandoned buildings.

*When blood is nipp'd and ways be foul,
Then nightly sings the staring owl,
Tu-who!*   Shakespeare

The long-eared owl's long 'ears' are only tufts of feathers on top of its head. Its real ears are on the side of its head. Sharp hearing and keen sight help it to find its prey.

Owls' eyes are placed in the front of their heads giving them good vision of distance and depth. Owls can also turn their heads almost completely round, so that they can see what is happening behind their backs.

*O was once a little owl
Owly
Prowly
Howly
Owly
Browny Fowly
Little Owl!*
Edward Lear

61

Scant is the holly,
The holly-berries few,
There's a bunch for the rich man
To see his Christmas through,
And a spray or a sprig
For the pretty well-to-do.

But what of the brown birds
Whom hunger maketh bold?
What of the poor birds
A-seeking in the cold?
Oh, when the holly's scant
And the holly-berries few,
What will the brown birds,
The poor birds do?

Eleanor Farjeon

male house sparrows

Sparrows

Many birds fly to warmer lands before winter comes. Those that stay, like sparrows, have a hard time. To help keep warm they ruffle up their feathers: this creates a blanket of warm air between their skin and the cold outside.

By day sparrows look for food: grain, seeds, insects . . . or crumbs that people put out for them in winter.

At night they go back to sleep in the nests they built in spring. They like to nest in holes: house sparrows find them in buildings, tree sparrows in trees.

male or female tree sparrow

A bitter morning:
sparrows sitting together
without any necks.

J. W. Hackett

The birds are hungry

You can help birds in winter by putting food out for them on a bird table or window ledge.

*It was evening all afternoon.
It was snowing
And it was going to snow.
The blackbird sat
In the cedar-limbs.*
    Wallace Stevens

blackbird

*black on white
crow in snow
hunched
wet lump
on brittle branch
remembering
warmth
remembering corn*
    Gustave Keyser

robin

crow

*When winter frost makes earth as steel,
I search and search but find no meal,
And most unhappy then I feel.*

Thomas Hardy

Birds like scraps of fat and cooked meat, peanuts and even rotten apples.

starling

blue tit

Birds need water all year round: so remember to break the ice for them in the bird bath or garden pond.

To give little birds a chance, spread food widely or hang some from a branch or by a window. Otherwise the bold greedy birds, like starlings and magpies, will get it all.

magpie

In Spring I look gay deck'd in comely array,
In Summer more clothing I wear;
When colder it grows, I fling off my clothes,
And in winter quite naked appear.

(a tree)

Planting a tree

Winter is the best time for tree planting, because then the sap is not flowing and the tree is at rest.

Of course many trees seed themselves in the wild. But others begin their lives by being reared in tree nurseries, and then transplanted to woods and gardens.

Tree roots need particular care in planting. They must have plenty of room to spread themselves (1). When the tree is in (2), the earth must be well packed round the roots (3). Then they must be watered (4).

Young trees are supported by stakes after planting (5).

And sometimes their trunks are protected with special covers to stop hungry animals, like rabbits, from nibbling the bark.

Oh the oak and the ash
And the bonny ivy tree
They are blooming
At home in my own country.

Anon.

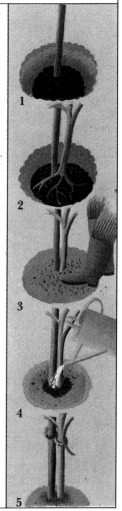

Even the bare trees of winter can be recognised because their shapes are so different.

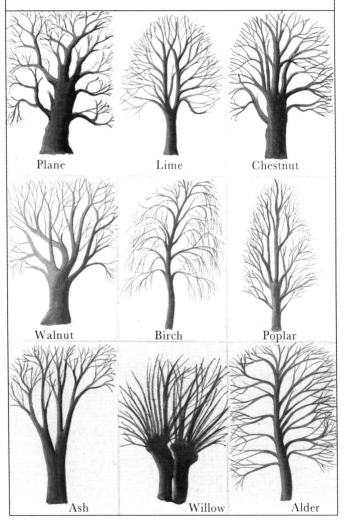

Plane

Lime

Chestnut

Walnut

Birch

Poplar

Ash

Willow

Alder

Trees without their leaves

The Oak

All his leaves fallen at length,
Look, he stands, trunk and bough,
Naked strength.

Tennyson

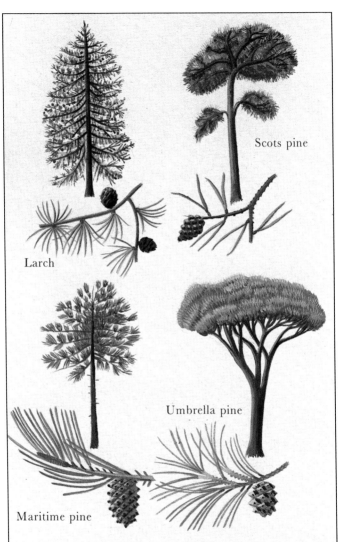

Scots pine

Larch

Umbrella pine

Maritime pine

Conifers get their name because most have cone-shaped fruit. Nearly all conifers are **evergreen.** The larch is an exception: it loses its leaves in autumn.

70

Spruce

Cedar

Cypress

Yew

The leaves of conifers are shaped like scales or needles. They have a waxy surface which protects them from the cold.

Today they cut down the oak.
Strong men climbed with ropes
in the brittle tree.
The exhaust of a gasoline saw
was blue in the branches.

It is February. The oak has been
dead a year.
I remember the great sails of its
branches
rolling out greenly, a hundred and
twenty feet up,
and acorns thick on the lawn.
Nine cities of squirrels lived in that
tree.
Today they run over the snow
Squeaking their lamentation.

Donald Hall

72

Woodcutting

A tree falls the way it leans.

On farms, winter is the season for woodcutting: there is least to be done in the fields then. In big forests trees are felled all year round.

Chainsaws driven by petrol have generally taken the place of the axe and handsaw. And there are now machines which can drive into the forest, fell the trees and cut them into logs.

73

Pruning

A gardener can alter the shape of a tree by pruning.

Trees and shrubs are pruned before they start to grow again with the rising of the sap in spring.

Pruning means cutting back. When a bud, tip or branch is cut back the one next to it will grow more. Dead and old branches are cut back to allow new ones to grow strong.

Fruit trees are often cut to make them branch out sideways against a garden wall, instead of growing upwards. This makes them yield more fruit, and the fruit is easier to pick.

It is important to leave plenty of buds when pruning. From them new shoots and flowers will emerge in the spring.

Trees produce buds in summer. Through the winter the buds rest, protected by tough brown water-proof scales which overlap like tiles on a roof. Underneath are smaller green scales and inside these a layer of soft woolly down which protects the young shoot. In spring each shoot will open out into a flower or leaves and a twig.

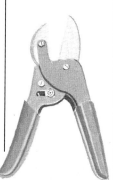

Secateurs

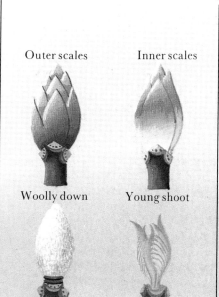

Outer scales   Inner scales

Woolly down   Young shoot

Pruning knife

Ivy

Ivy is an evergreen plant which, like the fir tree and the other evergreens, was considered magical.

Ivy, like holly and mistletoe, was believed to protect people against witches or demons. It was also the plant sacred to the Roman god of wine.

Ivy leaves, like those of many evergreens, have a glossy waxy surface. This protects them from drying out in cold weather when sap does not rise from the earth.

Ivy is a climbing plant and grows up walls or trees in shady places. It can harm trees by drawing nourishment from the earth around their roots, but it does not feed on the trees themselves.

In October or November ivy bears the last flowers of the year, providing food for insects which are soon to die in the cold. In winter it gives shelter to hibernating insects and its berries are eaten by hungry birds.

Lichen and moss

Lichens are strange plants. They are green, grey or yellow and grow in freezing conditions as well as in the desert, where no other plant would survive. They grow very slowly: not even half an inch in a year, and are often very old. You find them clinging to rocks or tree trunks.

Moss has tiny leaves which feel like fur. There are many thousands of species. Most grow in damp shady places but others are found on dry rocks. Moss soaks up rain like a sponge.

Who saw the moss
Creep over the
stone?
I, said the gray fox,
All alone.

Margaret
Wise Brown

Mistletoe

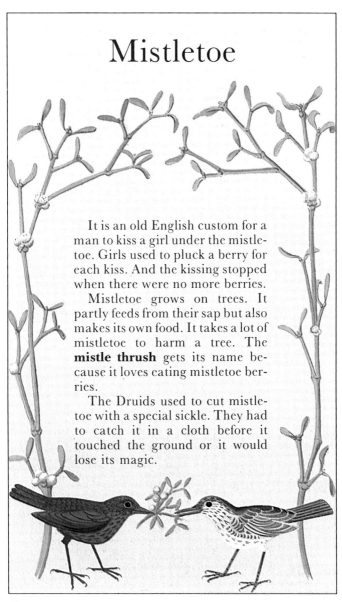

It is an old English custom for a man to kiss a girl under the mistletoe. Girls used to pluck a berry for each kiss. And the kissing stopped when there were no more berries.

Mistletoe grows on trees. It partly feeds from their sap but also makes its own food. It takes a lot of mistletoe to harm a tree. The **mistle thrush** gets its name because it loves eating mistletoe berries.

The Druids used to cut mistletoe with a special sickle. They had to catch it in a cloth before it touched the ground or it would lose its magic.

Holly

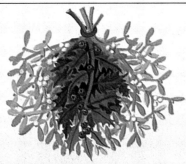

An old legend tells how holly got its berries. When the shepherds went to see Christ in the manger, they left a lamb behind. It was fenced in with thorns to keep out wolves. But the lamb, determined to follow them, pushed through the thorns and pricked itself. Drops of its blood froze and became holly berries.

The holly and the ivy,
When they are both full-grown
Of all the trees that are in the wood
The holly bears the crown.

A calendar of vegetables

Onion skin,
Very thin,
Mild weather
Coming in ...

There is still work to be done in the vegetable garden in winter: vegetables to pick, seeds to sow, seedlings to plant out. Seedlings are little shoots: they are first grown in a greenhouse or under a glass frame to

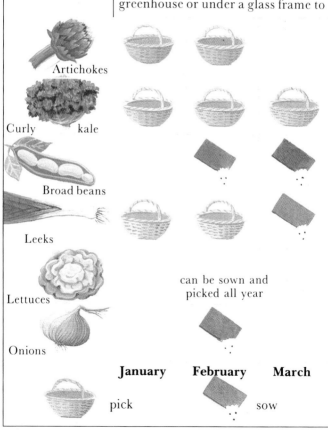

Artichokes

Curly   kale

Broad beans

Leeks

Lettuces

Onions

can be sown and
picked all year

January   **February**   **March**

pick   sow

protect them from the cold; then planted out when they are stronger and it is warmer. The dates given can vary by a few weeks. Vegetables grow earlier in warm areas and later in cold ones.

... Onion skin,
Thick and tough,
Coming winter
Cold and rough.

Anon.

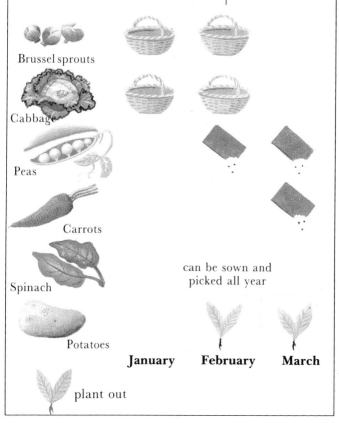

Brussel sprouts

Cabbage

Peas

Carrots

Spinach

can be sown and
picked all year

Potatoes

January   **February**   **March**

plant out

81

Gone were but the Winter,
Come were but the Spring,
I would go to a covert
Where the birds sing

Where in the whitethorn
Singeth a thrush,
And a robin sings
In the holly-bush.

Full of fresh scents
Are the budding boughs
Arching high over
A cool green house.

Christina Rossetti

In the fields of snow

In the new year, even before the snows have melted, new life begins to stir under the ground.

Buried seeds put out roots which anchor the new plants to the earth. Tips of new shoots emerge from the soil. Snow does not harm them. It protects the ground underneath from freezing.

When spring arrives, well-established plants will be ready to spurt into growth.

Green the young herbs
In the fields of snow,
Green, O, how green!

Raiza (Japanese)

The snows have scattered and fled; already the grass comes again.

Horace

Winter flowers

*Green bulbs
and spears and
slips
Promising oh
snowdrops
with double frills
of green and white,
Crocus of mauve
and gold.*

Eleanor Farjeon

The first flowers of the year bloom before the winter is over.

Snowdrops

The snowdrop likes to flower when the ground is cold. All summer its bulb draws nourishment from the earth, then waits until January or February to grow.

Christmas roses

Christmas roses get their name because they flower around Christmas. But they are not really roses.

Christmas rose

Daphne

I wonder if the sap is stirring yet,
If wintry birds are dreaming of a mate,
If frozen snowdrops feel as yet the sun,
And crocus fires are kindling one by one.
Christina Rossetti

Forsythia

The yellow flowers of the forsythia open before its leaves and are one of the brightest signs of the arrival of spring.

Crocus

Gold, mauve and yellow crocuses appear a little later, with the first thaw.

The yellow smell that blows
Across the air of meadows
Where bright forsythia grows.

Kathryn Worth

Forsythia

Snowdrop

Crocus

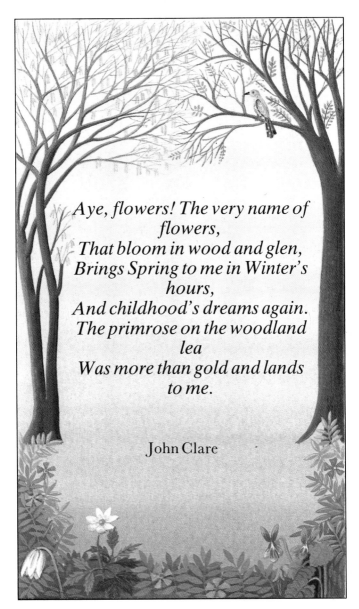

Aye, flowers! The very name of flowers,
That bloom in wood and glen,
Brings Spring to me in Winter's hours,
And childhood's dreams again.
The primrose on the woodland lea
Was more than gold and lands to me.

John Clare

The first butterfly

All winter long the **brimstone** butterfly hibernates, hiding under dead leaves or among the branches of a bush. Its body becomes stiff with cold and as brittle as glass.

In March, as the days grow warm, the brimstone awakes. It is the only butterfly at this time of year and feeds on the nectar of the first flowers.

Like a blossom from the sky,
Drops a yellow butterfly,
Dancing down the hedges grey
Snow-bestrewn till yesterday.

Frances Cornford

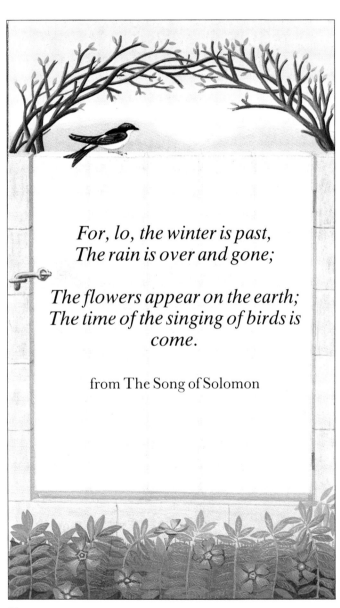

For, lo, the winter is past,
The rain is over and gone;

The flowers appear on the earth;
The time of the singing of birds is
come.

from The Song of Solomon

A winter dictionary

Avalanche
Avalanches are dangerous masses of snow that break away and rush down mountains, reaching speeds of up to 200 km per hour. They occur when too much snow piles up or when it thaws.

Befana
Befana is a good witch who brings presents to Italian children on 6 January.

Boxing Day
Apprentices used to collect money in Christmas boxes made of earthenware. Then they broke them open and shared their contents. This custom gave Boxing Day its name.

Christmas Pudding
Flour of England,
fruit of Spain,
Met together in
a shower of rain;
Put in a bag,
tied round
with a string
If you tell me
this riddle,
I'll give you a ring.

Collop Monday
On the Monday before Lent people used to eat collop, an old word for bacon and egg.

December
December gets its name from *decem*, the Latin word for ten. It was the tenth month of the old Roman calendar. The Anglo-Saxons called it Winter-Month or Holy Month because Christmas fell then.

Eskimos
Eskimos live in Greenland, Alaska and North Canada

where winters are long and snowy. Snow reflects sunlight, like a mirror. The dazzle can cause snow-blindness. To protect their eyes Eskimos wear glasses made of bone, wood or ivory with two slits to let in only a little light.

February
The Anglo-Saxons called February Sprout-kale Month because kale, or cabbage, grew then, and little else.

Glacier
In very cold regions snow stays all year without melting. It piles up and turns into a mass of ice which moves very, very slowly downhill, until it melts on reaching warmer temperatures. This is a glacier.

Gull
The black-headed gull is commonly seen in town parks. But it is often not recognised because in winter its chocolate-brown head turns white. Gulls from northern and eastern Europe come to England for the winter.

Hogmanay
At Hogmanay, the Scottish New Year, people go 'first-footing': they visit friends, taking cake, bread or coal.

Icebergs
Icebergs are huge pieces of ice which float in the sea, having broken away from glaciers at the north or south poles. They can be very dangerous for ships and sailors fear them. Only ⅛th of an iceberg shows above the water and they are often shrouded in mist.

Igloo
Igloo is the Eskimo word for house or shelter. On hunting expeditions Eskimos make igloos out of bricks of ice cemented with snow. The roofs are domes with a small hole in the top for air. Sometimes windows are made out of sheets of ice.

January

January is named after Janus, a Roman god. He had two faces: one looking back to the old year, the other forward to the new. The Anglo-Saxons called the month Wolf-month: hungry wolves then raided villages in search of prey.

Kolya, Kolya,
On Christmas Eve,
when all is still,
He puts his cakes
on the windowsill.

Kolya (St Nicholas) used to bring cakes to every Russian household on Christmas Eve.

Laurel

The tree we know as the common laurel is in fact an evergreen cherry. The true laurel is the bay laurel, or sweet bay, which comes from the Mediterranean. It is a symbol of victory. And its leaves are also used in cooking.

Little Owl

This is the owl you are most likely to see: it commonly flies by day as well as by night, and likes to sit on telegraph wires and poles. At dawn and dusk it hunts for rodents and small birds.

March

March was the month of Mars, the Roman god of war. The Anglo-Saxons called it Loud or Stormy Month.

Meat

When people were forbidden to eat meat in Lent, they used to salt it on Collop Monday so that it would keep until Lent was over.

Mince Pies

Mince pies used to be made with meat: a mixture of beef tongue, chicken, raisins, eggs, sugar and spices.

New Year

The Romans made midnight,
31 December the beginning of the new year. But some peoples celebrate new year at other times.

The Persian new year, for example, is the first day of spring.

Ring out the old,
ring in the new,
Ring, happy bells,
across the snow:
The Year is going,
let him go:
Ring out the false,
ring in the true.
                    Tennyson

Noel
This is an old cry of joy celebrating Christmas and still used in carols. Noel is also the French word for Christmas.

North Pole
There is no land at the north pole, but a thick layer of ice on the ocean.

Oranges
Oranges were once a rare treat which used to be given to children at Christmas time with a few sweets.

Pies
Dame get up
and bake your pies
On Christmas day
in the morning.

Plough Monday
On the first Monday after Twelfth Night farmworkers returned to work after the Christmas holidays. They dressed up and dragged a decorated plough through the village.

Quarter days
There are four quarter days in the year: 25 December, 25 March, 24 June, 29 September.

Raisins
On Christmas Eve people used to put raisins in a bowl and set them alight with brandy. Then everyone tried to pick them out of the flames. This game was called Snap-Dragon.

For he snaps
at all that comes
Snatching at
his feast of plums,
Snip! Snap!
Dragon!

Skates
The earliest skates were made of bones shaped into runners

and strapped to the feet. They did not go as fast over the ice as modern skates, which are metal blades fixed to boots.

Trolls

In Scandinavia trolls are believed to come out on Christmas Eve to dance and feast.

Turkey

The turkey was brought to Europe from Mexico several hundred years ago. It is now our traditional Christmas dish. In the old days people ate boar's head.

Ulex

Ulex Europaeus, or gorse, is an evergreen shrub. It bears yellow flowers, mainly in the spring; but they may continue to appear late into the winter.

Valentine

14 February has been the feast of lovers through the ages.

Wassail

At Christmas people used to drink wassail: a hot mixture of ale, eggs, curdled cream, roasted apples, nuts and spices.

Xmas

X begins Christ's name in Greek: Xmas is an old abbreviation.

Yule-log

It was an old custom to burn a huge log to last from Christmas to 12th Night.

Zibeline

The zibeline, or sable, lives in snowy parts of Siberia and Japan. It has been hunted for its very valuable fur.

Biographies

Danièle Bour and her family moved from Paris a few years ago to settle in a small village in Lorraine in north-east France. There the quiet of their country life, feeding their hens, making bread, horse riding, forms a framework for her work in painting and illustration. As well as Danièle Bour herself, both her elder daughters are involved in drawing – the eldest is now an established illustrator in her own right (see *Your Cat* in the Discoverers series). The winters in Lorraine are long and snowy, and their crisp beauty has a special place in Danièle Bour's imagination. Clear, cold snowscapes feature again and again in the illustrations which have made her a well-known and distinguished illustrator in France, and now in England (among her other books published here are *Oleg, the snow-leopard* and the 'Little Brown Bear' series).

Laurence Ottenheimer taught history and geography for a few years before working in publishing, where she specialises in activity and information books for young children.

Alex Campbell studied English literature at Oxford. Now the mother of two young children, she enjoys working on children's books while they are at school. In her work on the four *Discoverers* Season books she has taken particular pleasure in the choosing of the poems.

Acknowledgements

The editor and publishers wish to thank the following for permission to use copyright material:

Addison-Wesley Publishing Co. Ltd. for *The Secret Song* by Margaret Wise Brown from Nibble Nibble; George Allen & Unwin Ltd. for *Wind* by J. R. R. Tolkien from The Hobbit; John Baker Ltd. for *After the Japanese of Raizu* from Rainbows, Fleas & Flowers: A Nature Anthology (ed. Geoffrey Grigson); Curtis Brown Ltd. on behalf of the Estate of Ogden Nash for *Winter Morning, A Word About Winter* by Ogden Nash from Parents Keep Out, and for *The Stump* by Donald Hall; Dennis Dobson for *All Sorts* by Leonard Clark from Collected Poems and Verses; E. P. Dutton & Co. Inc. for *The Happy Hedgehog* by E. V. Rieu from The Flattered Flying Fish and Other Poems; Faber and Faber Ltd. for *Season Song* translated from the Irish by Flann O'Brien from The Rattle Bag, ed. Seamus Heaney & Ted Hughes, and for *The Heron, The Thought Fox* by Ted Hughes from The Hawk in The Rain, and for *13 Ways of Looking at a Blackbird* by Wallace Stevens from Selected Poems; Michael Joseph Ltd. for *Sparrows, The Tired Tree* by Eleanor Farjeon from Silver-Sand and Snow; Alfred A. Knopf for *January* by John Updike for A Child's Calendar; John Lehmann Ltd. for *Christmas Landscape* by Laurie Lee from The Bloom of Candles; The Literary Trustees of Walter de la Mare for *Snow* by Walter de la Mare from Collected Works; McNatt, Josephine Curry for *Smells* by Kathryn Worth from Poems for Josephine (Random House Book of Poetry for Children, sel. Jack Prelutsky); Julia MacRae Books for *The Ants and the Grasshopper* trans. Harold Jones; Methuen Books Ltd. for *Furry Bear* by A. A. Milne from Now We Are Six; Oxford University Press for *Christmas Tree* by Laurence Smith for The Oxford Book of Christmas Poems, ed. Michael Harrison & Christopher Stuart-Clark, and for *31 December* by Eleanor Farjeon from The New Book of Days; Charles Scribner's Sons for *Moles* by Aileen Fisher from Cricket in a Thicket; University of Mexico Press for *Absolutes* by Gustave Keyser from New Mexico Quarterly, Autumn 1963; Ure Smith Sydney for *The Song of the Year* by Irene Gough from One Sunday Morning Early; Weekly Reader, Xerox Educational Publications for *The Chickadee, Frosty Window, There Goes Winter* by Aileen Fisher from Out in the Dark and Daylight (Harper & Row).

Every effort has been made to trace copyright but if any omissions have been made please let us know in order that we may put it right in the next edition.